# Helmut **Newton**

Introduction by Karl Lagerfeld

with comments by Helmut Newton

**Thames & Hudson** PHOTOFILE

*The Photofile series is the original English-language
edition of the Photo Poche collection. It was conceived and
produced by the Centre National de la Photographie, Paris.
Robert Delpire is the creator and managing editor of the series.*

First published in the United Kingdom in 1989 by
Thames & Hudson Ltd, 181A High Holborn, London WC1V 7QX

www.thamesandhudson.com

Published in 2006 in paperback in the United States of America by
Thames & Hudson Inc., 500 Fifth Avenue, New York, New York 10110

thamesandhudsonusa.com

Originally published in France by Centre National de la Photographie
Copyright © 2004 Actes Sud, Arles
Photographs © Helmut Newton
English translation copyright © 1987 Centre National de la Photographie
This edition © 1989, 2006 Thames & Hudson Ltd, London

British Library Cataloguing-in-Publication Data
A catalogue record for this book is available from the British Library

Library of Congress Catalog Card Number 2005908450

ISBN-10:  0-500-41069-0
ISBN-13:  978-0-500-41069-1

Printed and bound in France

# 'NORDFLEISCH'

Some years ago, Helmut Newton happened to be in Hamburg. One evening, while taking a walk along the docks, his eye was caught by the sign over a meat warehouse that said 'Nordfleisch' – meat from the north. That seemed to him to sum up his work. And that's why I chose it as the title for this introduction.

Newton's preference for 'pale' skin is so strong that when he wants – or has – to photograph nudes in colour, he mixes in a blue light with the tungsten lighting to eradicate the warm tones that he doesn't like. He would like to take colour shots accidentally; he even pretends that he doesn't know he has colour film in his camera.

He says he likes cold women – another reason for the above title. But the word is not to be construed as intimidating cold indifference. He simply wants the presence of his models to be somewhat abstracted from the circumstances or surroundings. For him, 'cold' is the opposite of 'romantic' and 'sentimental' – two adjectives that are foreign to him, even thoroughly detestable. In writing about Newton and his work, you have to forget those two words. He clearly doesn't care for long descriptions and complicated analyses; he says, 'Those who write about photography write only for those who write about photography.'

I have read some extravagant and far-fetched articles on his work, phrased in terms that were in vogue during art's 'lyric abstraction' period. Yet nothing is less abstract than Newton's women. If he had to think about all the subtle motivations that he is credited for in his work, he would be paralysed and couldn't do anything. Hence his indifference to critics and what they say. 'The only thing I care about,' he says, 'is that they get my name right.' He has only one answer for those who are scandalized by his photos: 'You've got to be able to live up to something, even a bad reputation.'

In his photos there is no mockery, no disdain. He does not try to make women look ridiculous. He has his own very particular way of idealizing a reality which is not always ideal. This, however, is the source of his inspiration. (One day, Matisse asked Maillol why all his sculpted figures had thick masses of hair. 'Because Madame Maillol does,' replied the sculptor.) He takes female destiny very seriously. For him, neither sex is weaker. Yet feminists despise him. Young, socially militant photographers accuse him of being the lackey of the consumer society. But he is only describing what he knows and what he sees.

Helmut Newton admits that he feels very comfortable in Paris, New York, Berlin, Los Angeles, the French Riviera – all the places the jet set prefers. What he likes about Los Angeles is the city of Los Angeles. When he is there, if he is supposed to photograph a woman in a car, the car has to be an American one, a Cadillac. In Berlin, it's a Mercedes. In Paris, a Citröen. He himself arrived in Paris in 1956 at the wheel of a white Porsche with red leather seats.

For me, his life is a like a triptych. In the first panel, there is Berlin, his childhood, his spiritual home. Next, his Australian period, which is mysterious and unknown. And, lastly the period that started 25 years ago when he drove into Paris in his Porsche. Paris has become his home port, although he lives in the south of France, and spends a lot of time travelling. Paris is one of those rare cities that people easily adopt even if they haven't grown up there. He shares the sentiment of the German writer Tucholsky, who spoke of the 'infinite happiness of being able to live in Paris.' Today, he would amend that statement to include Monte Carlo.

I can easily picture the boy who lived in Berlin during the thirties. That's one of the reasons I enjoy our conversations so much. They sometimes go on for hours. He's a wonderful storyteller. From 1936 to 1938 he worked in Berlin as an apprentice to Yva, a famous photographer in those days, whose portraits and fashion photos are known to very few. But for me, Newton is first of all the schoolboy of *The Blue Angel*, blowing on the feathered skirt pasted on the picture postcard of Lola Lola (Marlene Dietrich).

It's a shame he was too young at the time to photograph Marlene – it would have been marvellous. Actually, he almost did, in 1972. Francine Crescent, then editor-in-chief of French *Vogue*, had asked me to introduce him to Miss Dietrich so that he could shoot a few pictures of her. This happened shortly after he'd suffered a mild heart attack in New York. In the elevator taking us up to Marlene's apartment on Avenue Montaigne, he was as excited as a kid and was telling me how important she'd been in his erotic daydreams when he was younger. The introduction went well. Then we started talking about illness and medicine – two of Marlene's favourite subjects. She was wearing a tight-fitting jersey top and a leather wraparound skirt. She jumped up and undid the snaps of her skirt. I'll never forget Helmut's surprise at this unexpected strip. He blurted out, 'The legs are still wonderful!' This really irritated Marlene, and so there were no photos. Too bad.

Although Newton built his reputation as a fashion photographer, his photos have survived the styles they illustrated. He was smart enough to avoid the cliché of the fashion photographers of the sixties. With time, his own image, like his photos, has become more audacious, while the *enfants terribles* from those days have melded into an amorphous, anonymous mass. Because he is quickly bored, he never repeats himself; he's always looking for something new. Once they reach a certain level, a lot of photographers produce the same picture over and over again, because they think their style has peaked and that that's what the public wants. On the other hand, you don't have to be an expert to recognize a photo by Newton at first glance, even though he never takes the same picture twice. His 'periods' are shorter and shorter. That's why he'll always stay with the fashion world – he likes change too much. For him, art for art's sake is a sterile concept. Francine Crescent risked her job at *Vogue* by printing his photos at a time when no other fashion magazine dared. It's true that ten years ago, readers were less blasé and more easily shocked than they are today.

For Newton, fashion is a familiar world where he has found his natural expression. He loves everything that is artificial. 'Everything that is beautiful is fake,' he says. 'The most beautiful lawn is plastic.' These two mottoes are from his notes. Because he can't draw, he jots down everything he wants to include in his new photos. He uses a telegraphic style that no one else can decipher, scribbling ideas on pages among the telephone numbers, hotel addresses, dates, and appointments he's already noted. These notes are the backbone of his work discipline. The word 'discipline' often dominates his vocabulary both at work and in his private life. Yet he contends that he loves to be lazy. In fact, his laziness helps him to recharge the batteries of his imagination and protects him from a corrosive routine.

I think that the anti-Newtons are fewer and farther between nowadays. To denounce his photos as vulgar or pornographic borders on the ridiculous. The same thing was said about the Impressionists and later about the Expressionists. The works of

Manet, Renoir, Toulouse-Lautrec, Beckmann and Dix, which caused such a furore when exhibited for the first time, now hang in museums. I'm positive that Helmut Newton will have a place of honour in a future museum of photography. The danger in his photos are that they are insidious – they insinuate themselves into and leave a lasting imprint on his detractors' imaginations. It's a very rare gift.

He often says that he takes pictures so they can be seen and not just to be thrown into a drawer. The concept of art should not kill the concept of artificiality, because that's where its artistic expression comes from. The photos in this book represent a decisive change in Newton's creativity. In his more recent work the framing and the setting, which usually are so important to him, incorporate two new elements: scale (for his monumental photos) and time (for the most recent). It's the famous 'nevermore' time that passes and never comes back. It isn't quite *Ave atque vale* (Hail and farewell), and it's more subtle than the quote from Shakespeare that he uses as a caption for the X-ray of a head with a necklace that is on the first page of one of his books: 'Golden lads and girls all must, as chimney-sweepers, come to dust.'

For him, the symbolism of the duplicate pictures shot at Brescia is very important. The same place – a Fascist-style villa by the sea, the same set-up, the same woman – clothed in one shot, nude in the other (but wearing high heels – that, for Newton, is true nudity). The second photo is almost exactly the same as the first. Just one thing is different: the light. The sunlight is no longer the same. The moment has moved on forever.

'Death prays on youth,' said Edith Sitwell in one of her songs of the Ivory Coast. In a certain way, I see his photos as an unconscious evocation of Wedekind's Lulu. I know he hates such anecdotal comparisons; his photos are not narratives (like those frivolous Italian romantic picture stories called *fumetti*). But these twinned photos are intensely dramatic. Newton claims that he is not telling a story. What he's interested in is the present moment. To show this ephemeral and unique aspect, he takes the same photo twice; the power and the meaning of the first is all the more compelling because the second take is different despite every effort to faithfully reconstruct the first. He had already used the same idea in a studio series he did for French *Vogue*. Studio light – unchanging, perfect – transforms models into store-window mannequins. The fragility of daylight is missing. Newton doesn't care much for studio work. In fact, his big photos of nudes on a white background are like the attempts at sculpture by certain great painters, like Modigliani, Renoir, and Degas, for whom models were so important.

Today, painting has run into so many dead ends that it seems to me that photography is the art form that best expresses our time. I am afraid that, as an art form, painting will come to a standstill like opera. The essential has been created. What we have to do is to keep photography from becoming 'established'. It has to stay alive.

Usually Newton works exclusively with professional models and hardly ever with men. I feel therefore all the more flattered that he has photographed me so often over the past twelve years. I've experienced the full gamut of emotions, sitting in front of his lens. You almost have the physical sensation of becoming a Newton. He himself is in a trance. Only his incredible technique lets him remain in control of the situation, even if he's mostly unaware of it. I imagine that when he photographs a nude woman, the atmosphere must be even more charged and intense.

He orders his victims about in German or English. Rarely, in French, although he has lived in France a lot longer than anywhere else. But French is probably a language that doesn't suit his universe. You have to have heard him say the German worlds *arsch* and *brust* in talking about the model's buttocks and breasts. French suddenly seems too weak, and you get the impression that the words are describing something else entirely.

Helmut Newton is still a foreigner, fascinated by the most mundane events of daily life in France. He loved going to the Luxembourg Gardens when he lived close by. Details that only a stranger is apt to notice would catch his attention. He has picked up a lot of ideas that way but he would never dream of photographing things on the spur of the moment. It is in recreating visual experience that the most ordinary things become aesthetic images.

There is never any trace of nostalgia in his photos. No one is more cosmopolitan than Newton; even his sophistication has roots. His past (or the idea that he has of it) has left its imprint on his very personal style. In fact, he lives within himself. His soul is his true spiritual home, a home that has nothing to do with the concept of homeland, but which has a good deal to do with the idea so neatly expressed in a Berlin song: 'Ich trab noch einen Koffer in Berlin' (I still have a trunk in Berlin).

This memory is the source of a talent that never looks back in time.

Some people consider his photos of orthopaedic equipment provocative. However, it was the neck brace that Erich von Stroheim wore in *La Grande Illusion* that gave him the idea. (Moreover, Erich von Stroheim reminds him of his father.) Although he was inspired by this actor-director, he never takes himself to be a director. What he's interested in is the image and not the story. Yet, in some of von Stroheim's films there are moments, sequences that come back to you, like Newton photos, but you don't recall the action. In *Foolish Wives* in particular, there are some very Newton-like scenes, which, moreover, take place in Monte Carlo, one of Newton's favourite haunts these days. The highly contrasted black and white sequence where von Stroheim is seducing the chamber-maid could be by Newton. And I'm not even sure that he ever saw the movie.

It's sometimes said of certain painters that they are 'a woman's painter'. The same notion can be applied to Newton – he is a 'woman's photographer'. But the photos that he takes of them are not necessarily those that people expect to see. In his own way he has transformed, or at any rate profoundly influenced, the erotic fantasies of our time. And his influence has spread farther than he thinks, making of him a sort of sorcerer's apprentice who has unleashed a perpetual flow of contemporary images. The secret of this power rests in that kind of detachment and distance that you feel women have. His models are no longer young girls even if often they are not yet twenty. He shows only adults, free and independent beings, women who, without necessarily looking like Gayle Olinekova or Lisa Lyon, exude self-assurance and complete determination.

What will the woman of the next century look like? Perhaps the answer to that can be found in the photos of Helmut Newton.

Karl Lagerfeld

Translated by Marianne Tinnell Faure

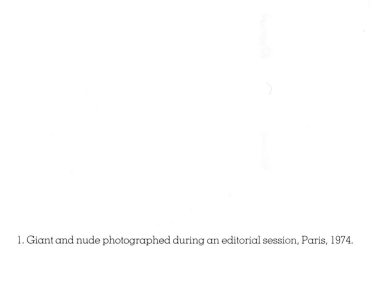
1. Giant and nude photographed during an editorial session, Paris, 1974.

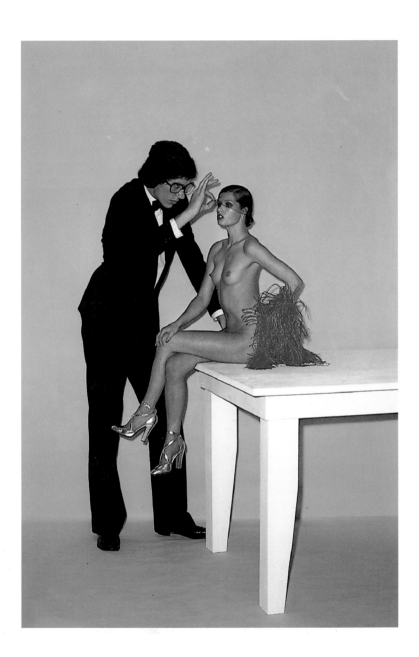

2. *Vogue* (Great Britain), 1968. London. Pourelle.

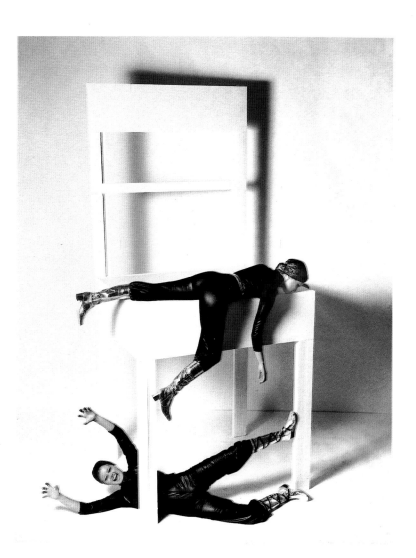

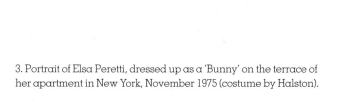

3. Portrait of Elsa Peretti, dressed up as a 'Bunny' on the terrace of her apartment in New York, November 1975 (costume by Halston).

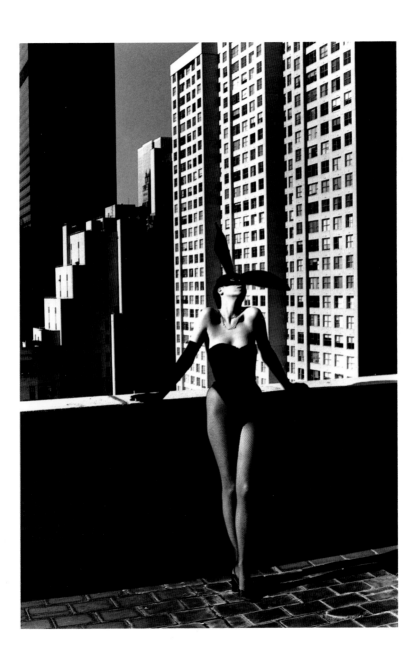

4. Central Park West, New York, 1975–78.

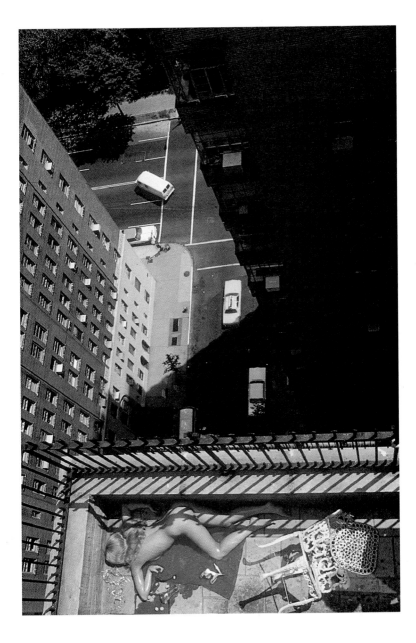

5. *Queen*, 1968. Paris. Jean Muir.

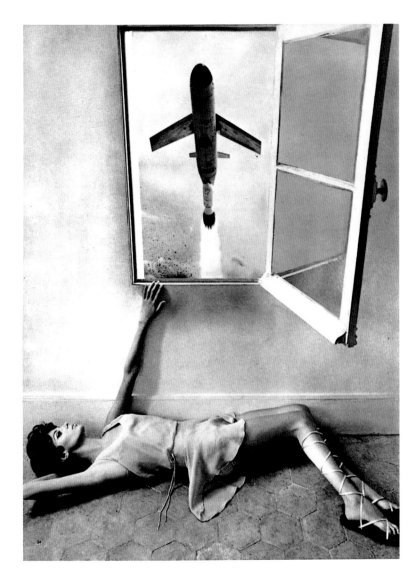

6. *Vogue* (USA), 1975. Saint-Tropez. Calvin Klein.

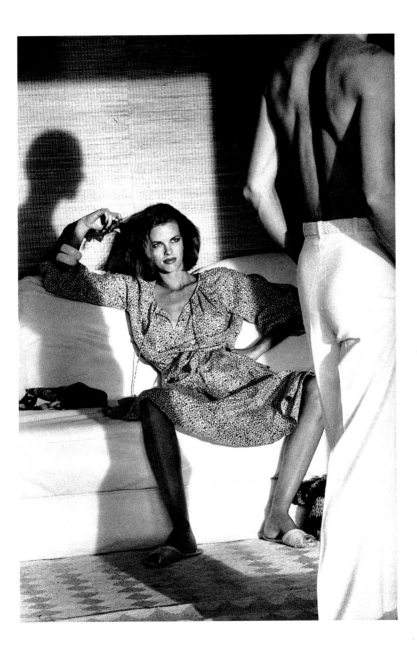

7. *Vogue* (France), 1978. From left to right: Arrabel, Arrabel, Azzaro.

Overleaf: 8. Swimming pool in a house in the suburbs, Melbourne, 1973.

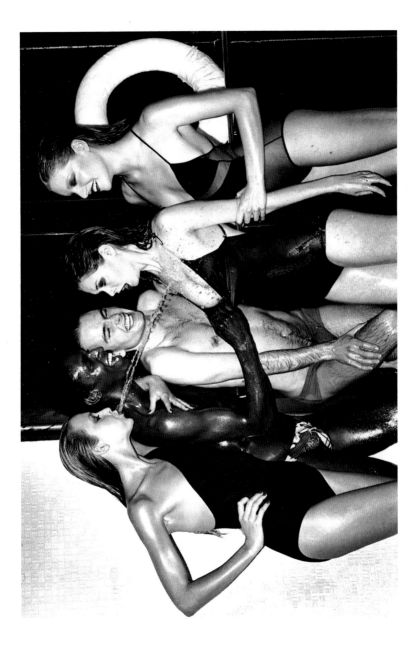

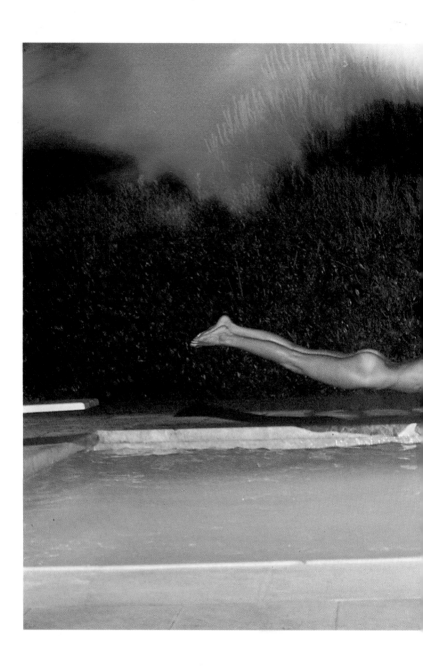

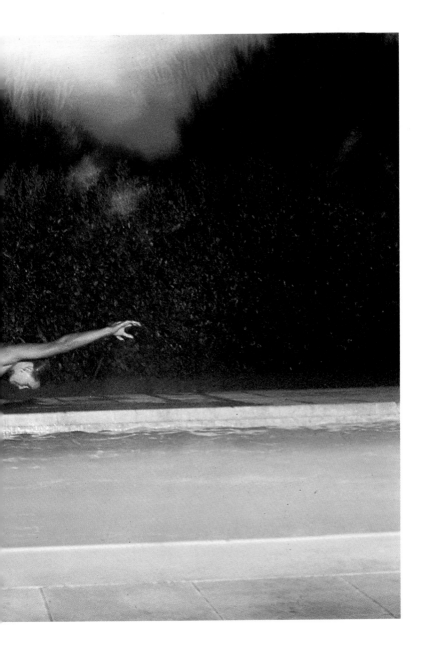

9. Laurie Livingston, Beverly Hills, 1981.

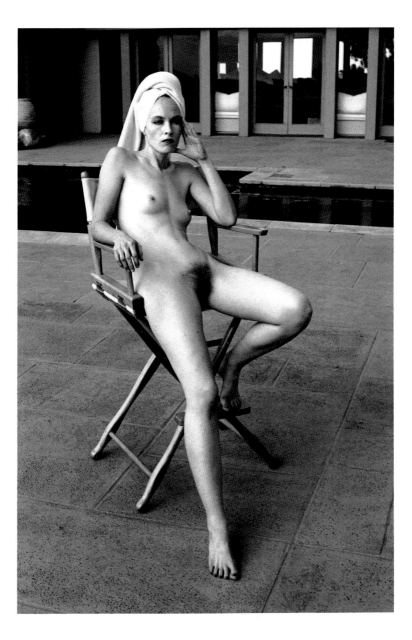

10. *Stern*. 1980. Cannes. Monica.

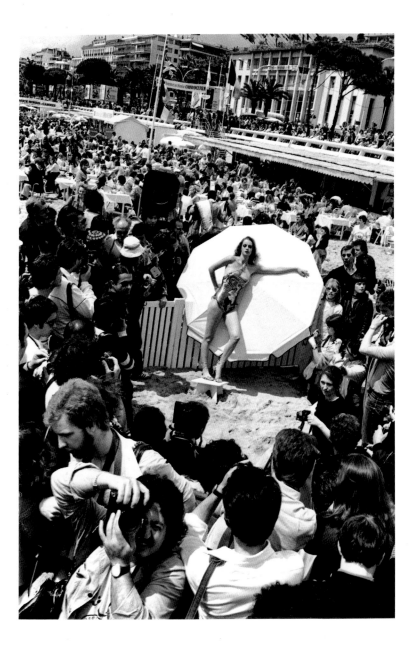

11. *Vogue* (France), 1981. Cannes. Hat: Jean Barthet.
Coat: Revillon. Swimsuit: Yvan & Marzia.

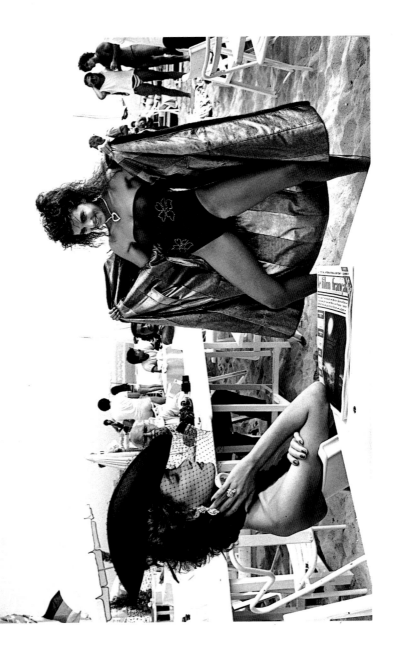

12. *Vogue* (USA), 1975. Miami. Rudi Gernreich.

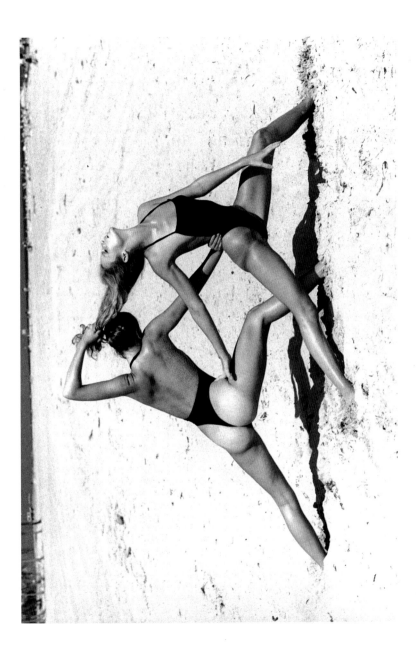

13. *Vogue* (France), 1978. Paris. Jean Patou and Guy Laroche.

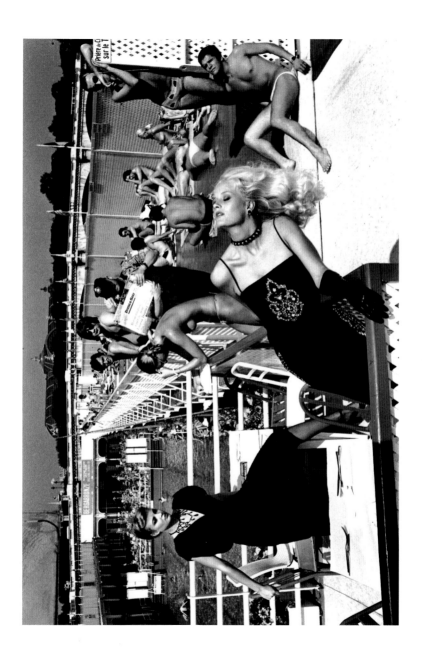

14. Saint-Tropez, June 1975.

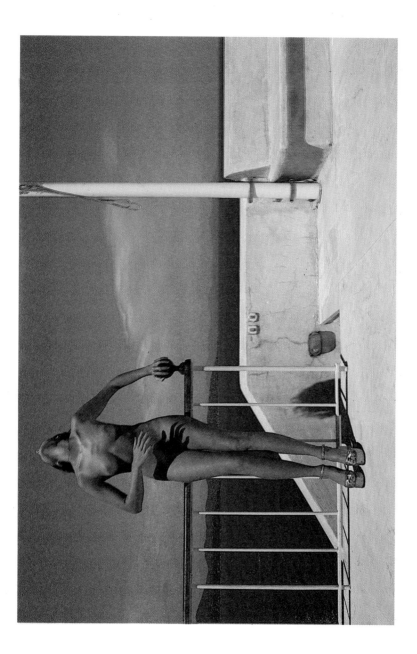

15. Margot, Beverly Hills, 1981.

Overleaf: 16. Weeping willow I, Weeping willow II, Ramatuelle, 1975–78.

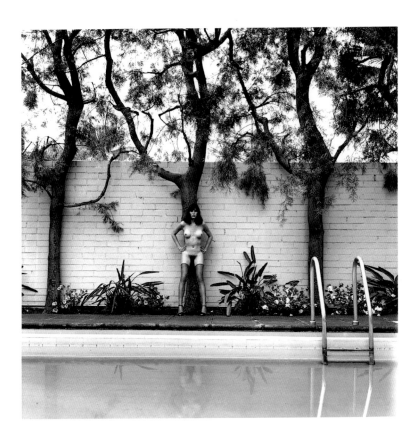

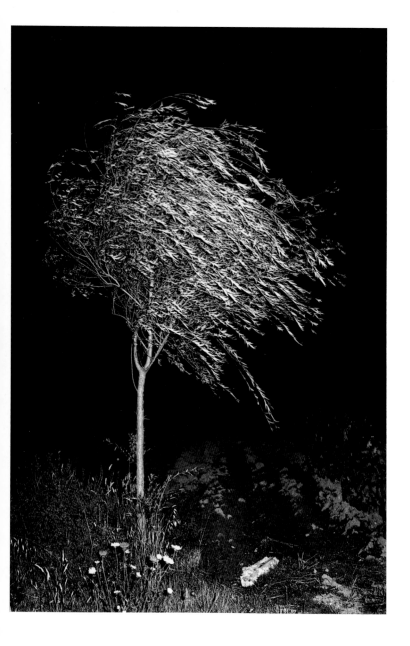

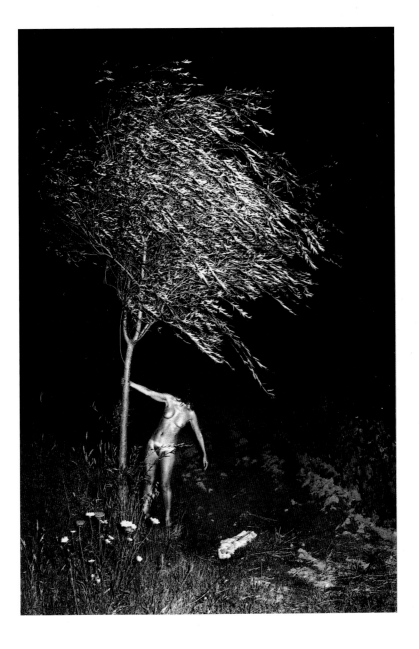

17. Nude in seaweed, Saint-Tropez, 1981.

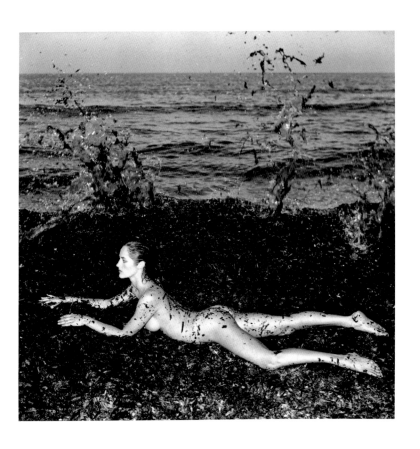

18. In a garden near Milan, 1975–78.

Overleaf: 19. Nastassja Kinski and her director,
James Toback, Hollywood, 1983.

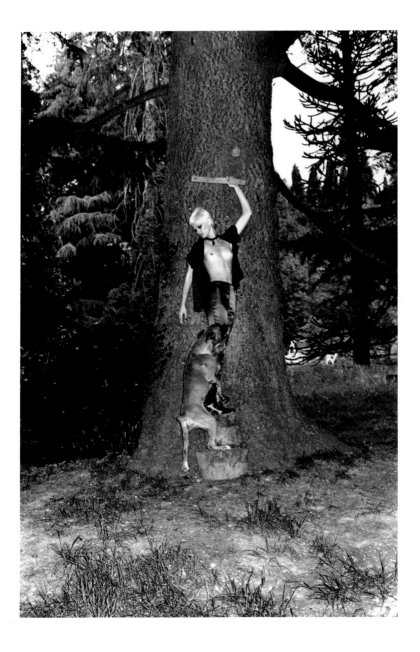

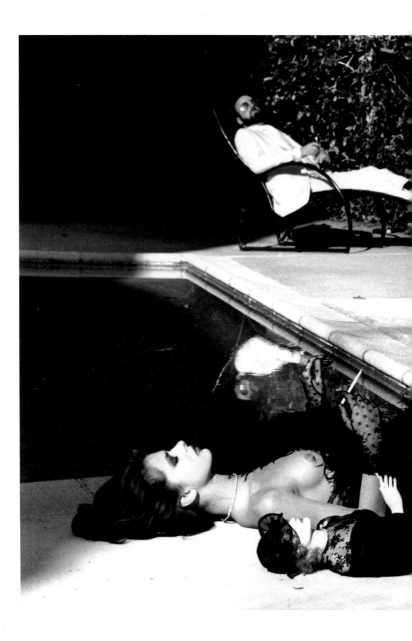

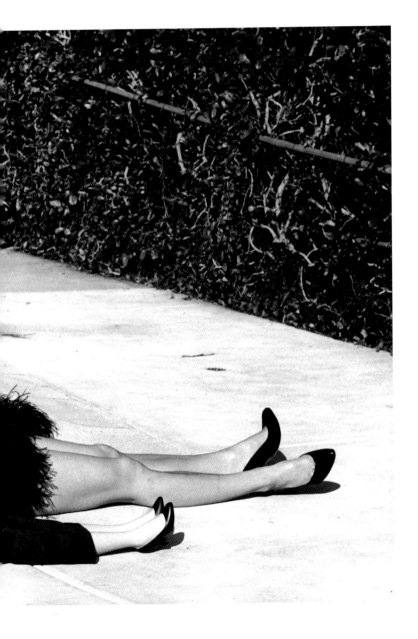

20. Nude descending a staircase, Nice, 1981.

Overleaf: 21. Parc de Saint-Cloud, Paris, 1974.

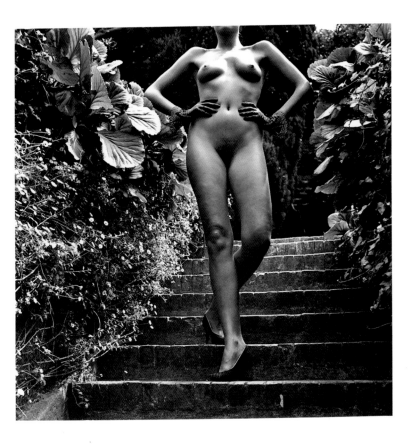

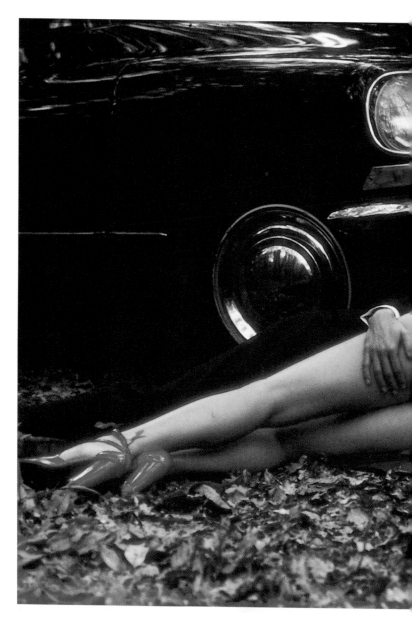

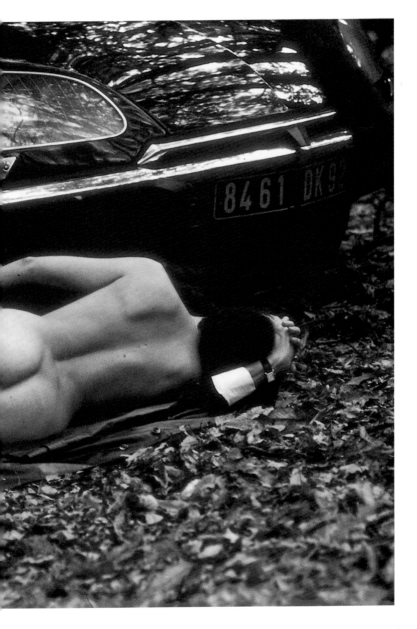

22. Berlin nude, 1975–78.

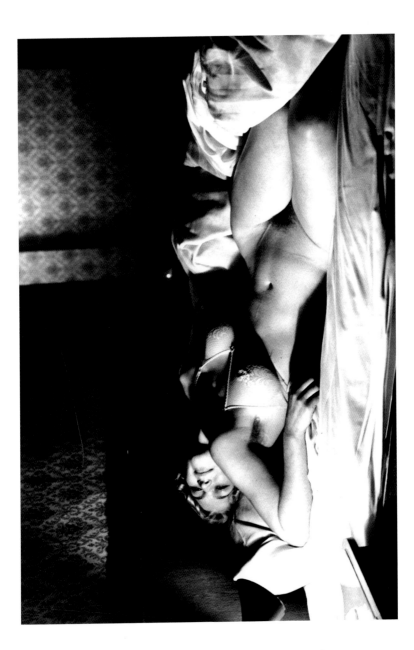

23. At Maxim's, first floor, Paris, 1975–78.

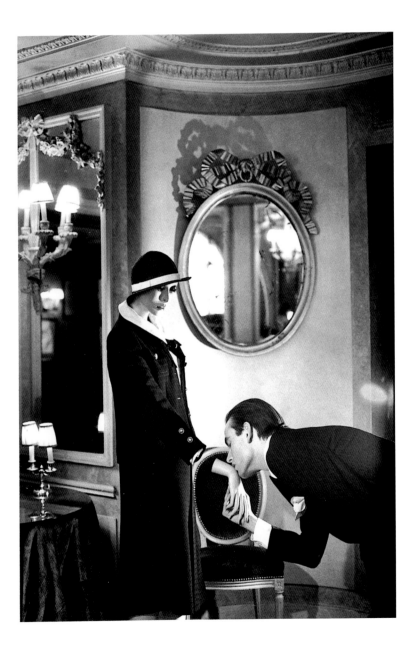

24. *Vogue* (France), 1978. Paris. Marc Bohan for Christian Dior.

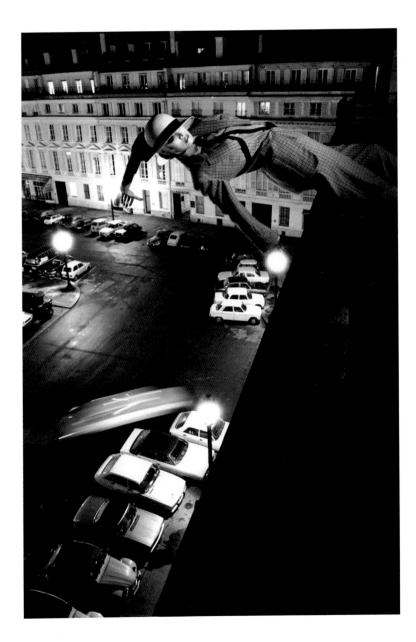

25. Bergstrøm above Paris, 1975–78.

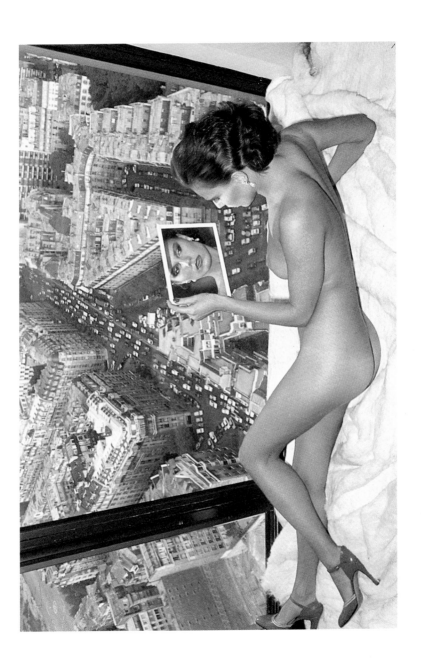

26. Queen, 1966. Paris. Grès.

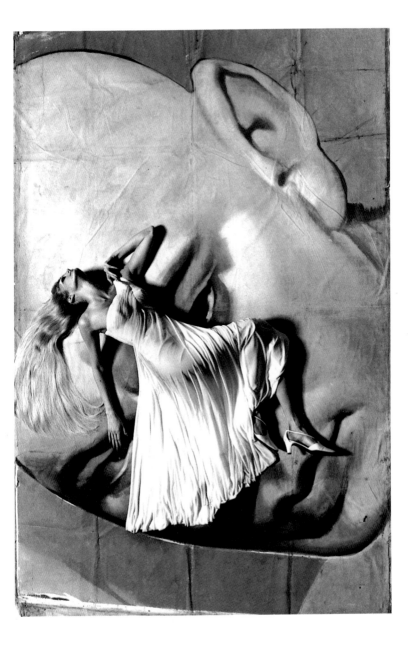

27. Lisa Lyon at home, Venice, California, 1981.

Overleaf: 28. Mrs Kiki Kiser on her court
and Mr Irving Blum II, Los Angeles, 1979.

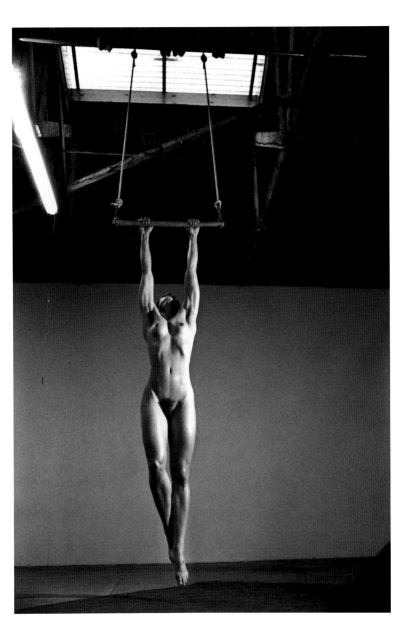

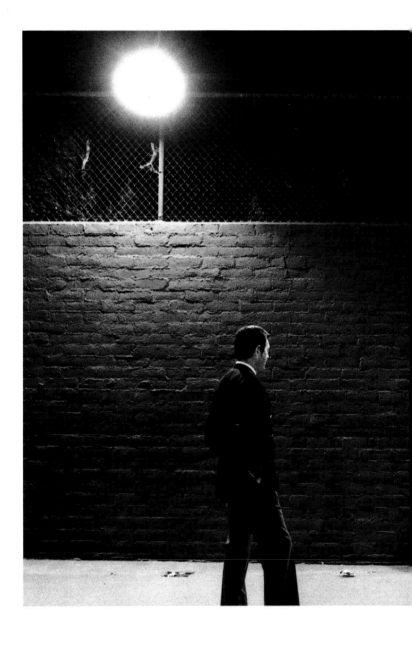

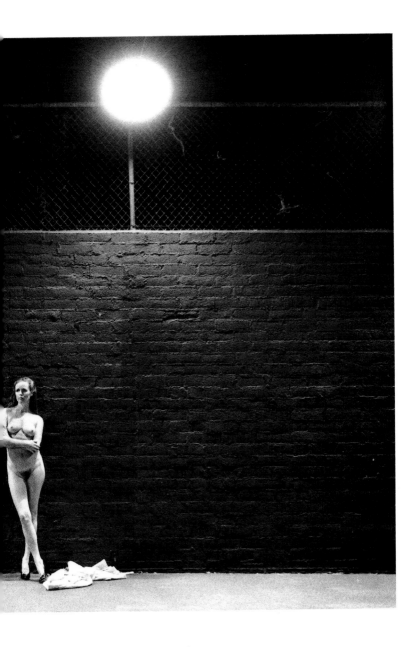

29. Big nude, I, 1980.

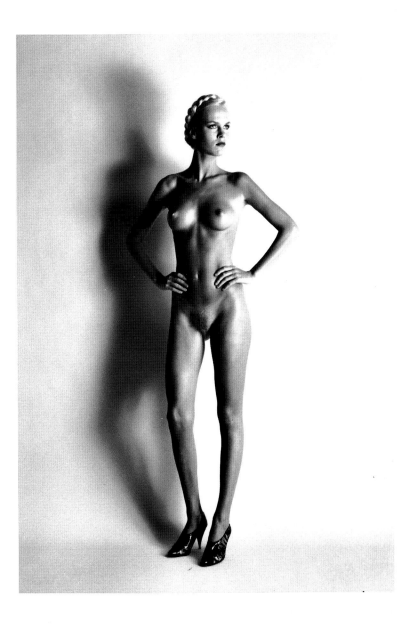

30. Brigitte Ariel in Oscar Wilde's bedroom. L'Hôtel, Paris, 1974.

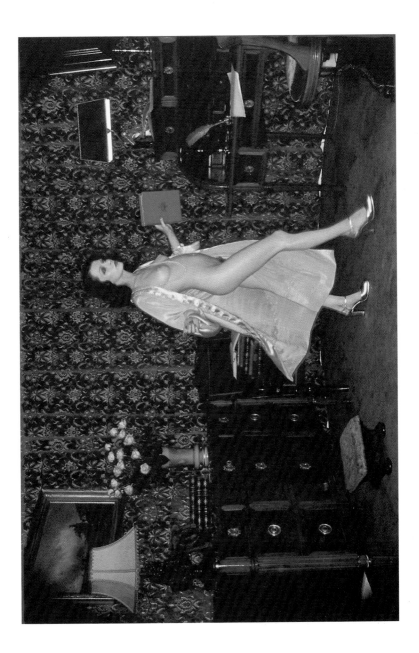

31. Masked nude with rubber stockings, Ramatuelle, 1981.

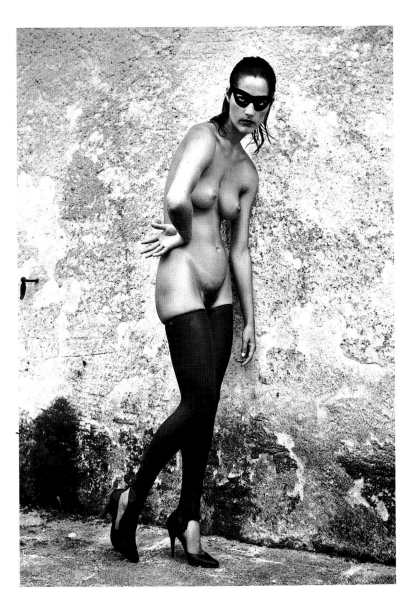

32. Queen, 1965, Paris.

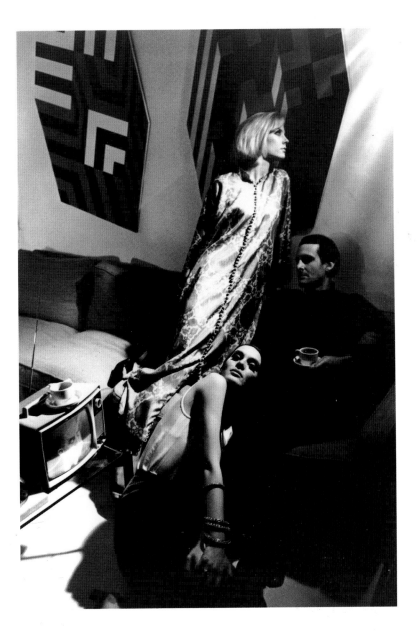

33. Department store mannequins I, 1975–78.

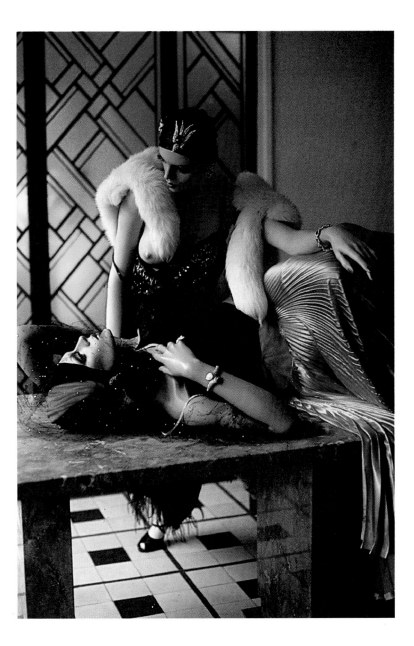

34. *Vogue* (France), 1980. Paris. Ungaro and Chanel.

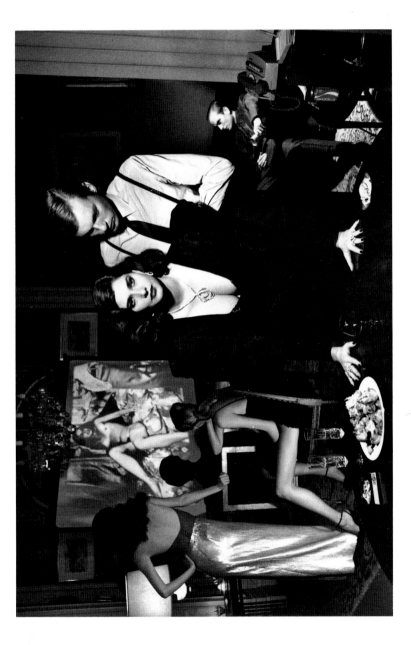

35. *Queen*, 1965. London.

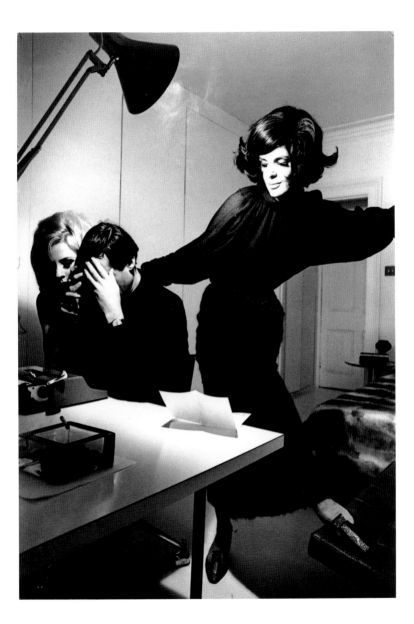

36. Jenny Capitän, Pension Dorian, Berlin, 1975–78.

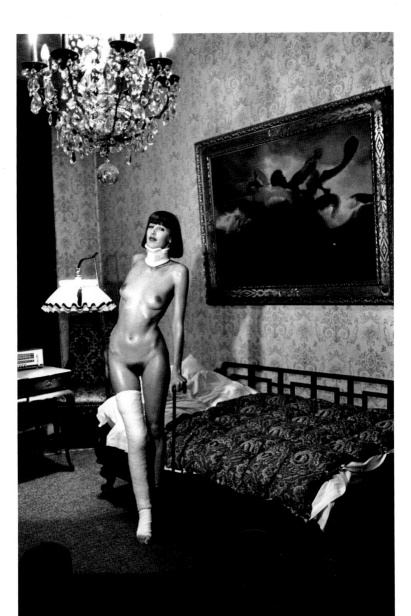

37. Princesse de Polignac, Paris, 1979.

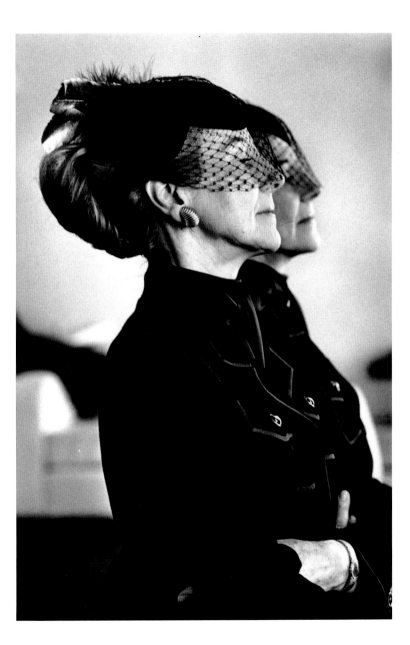

38. Mannequin and model I, 1975–78.

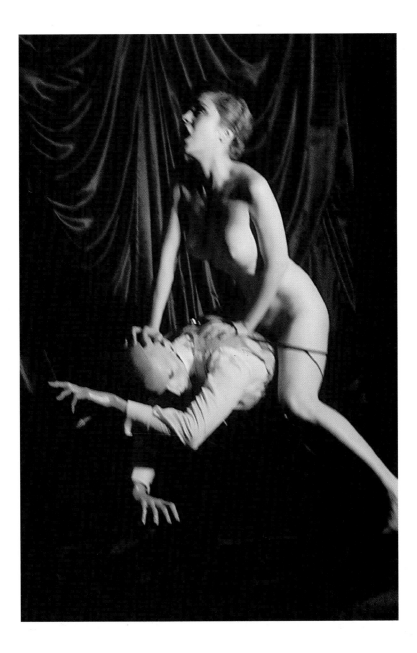

39. *Vogue* (France), 1979. Paris. Yves Saint Laurent.

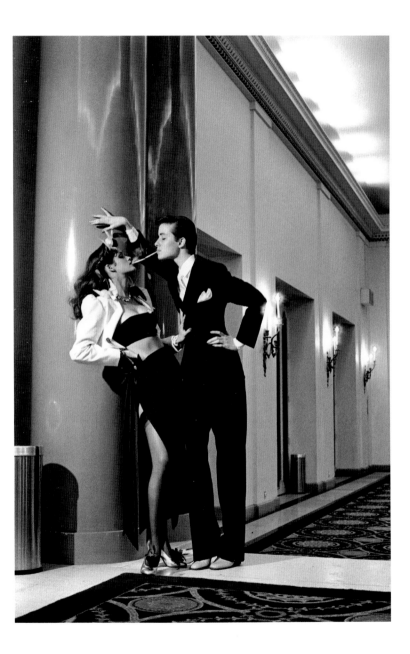

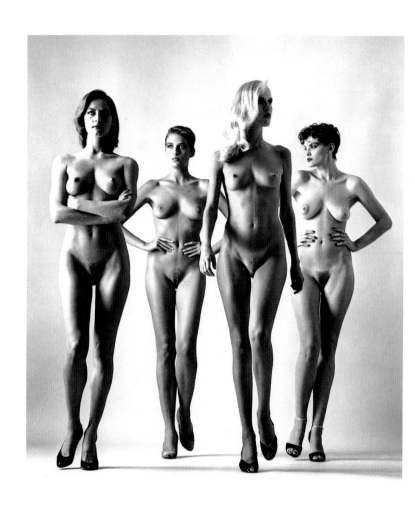

40. *Vogue* (France), 1981. 'The Unclothed and the Clothed'.

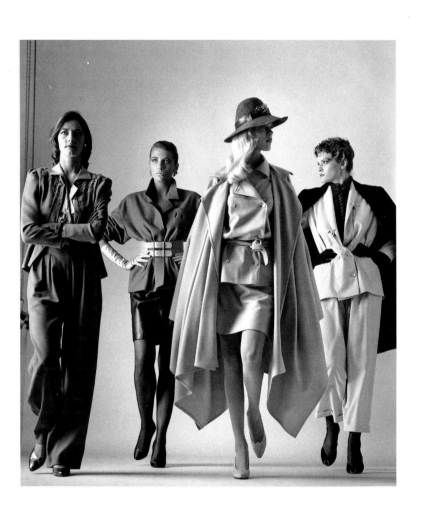

41. Sylvia in my studio, Paris, 1981.

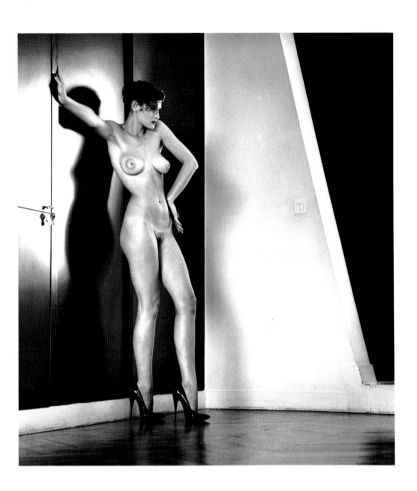

42. Portrait of Xavier Moreau and his girlfriend, Paris, 1974.

Overleaf: 43. *Vogue* (France), 1979. Paris.
Furs: Reby-Tigre Royal. Clothes: Milanka.

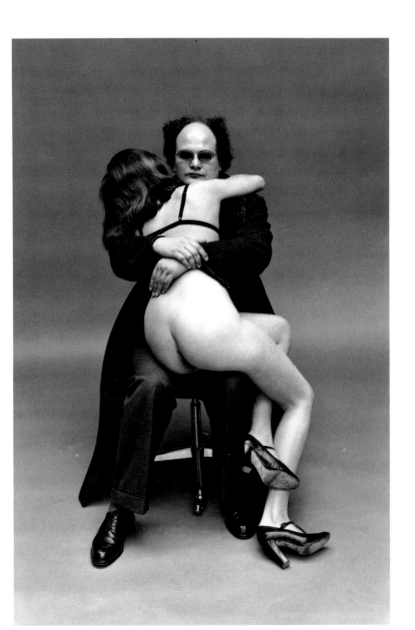

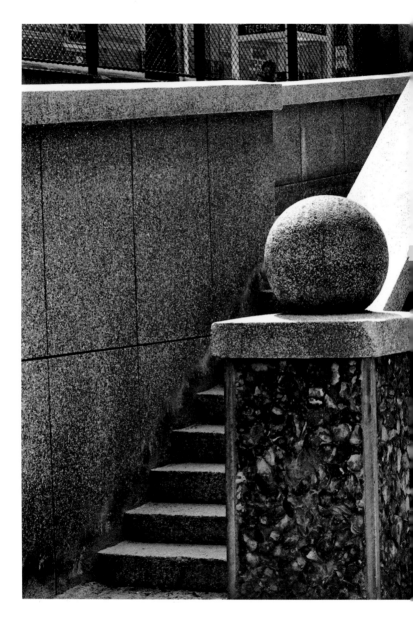

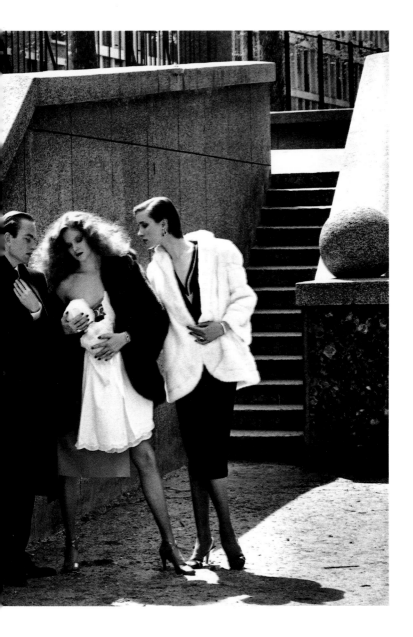

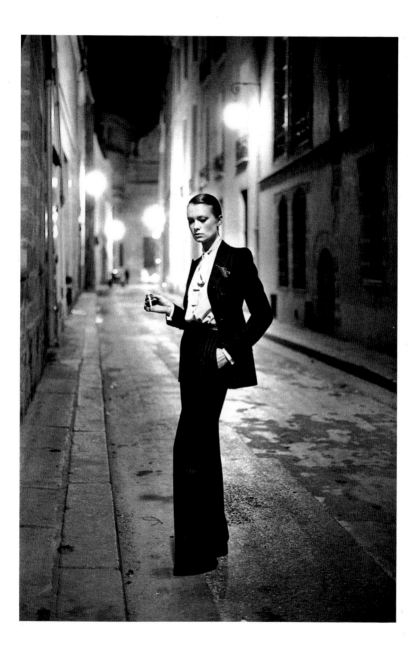

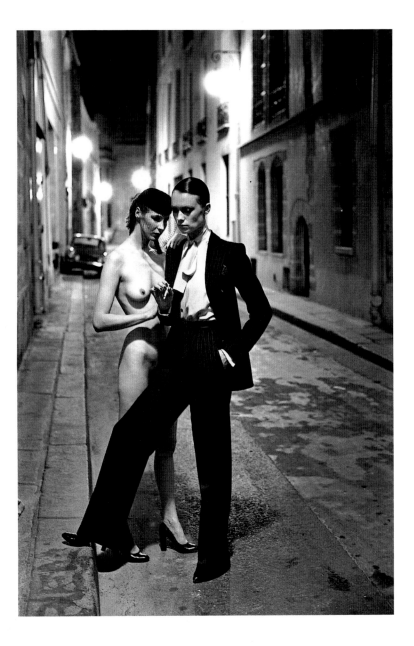

45. *Vogue* (France), 1981. Paris. Yves Saint Laurent.

Preceding pages: 44. *Vogue* (France), 1975. Paris. Yves Saint Laurent.

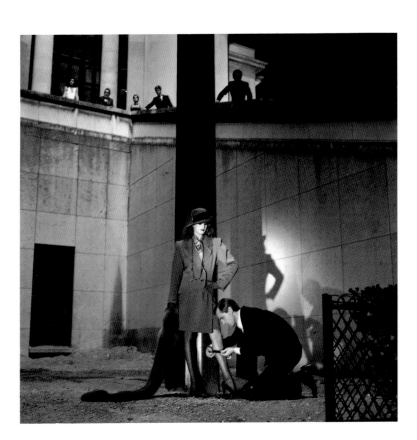

46. *Vogue* (France), 1974. Paris. Pierre Cardin.

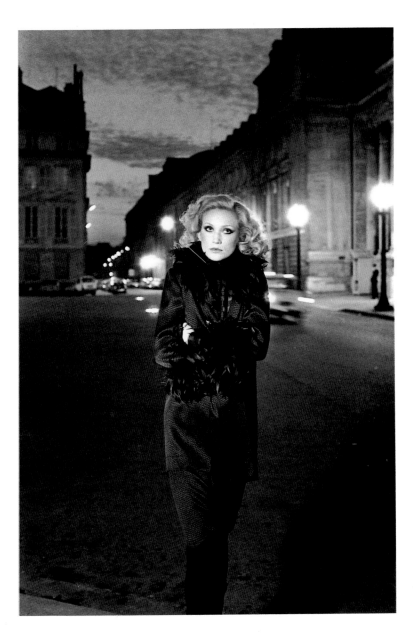

47. *Linea Italiana*, 1974. Rome. De Barentzen.

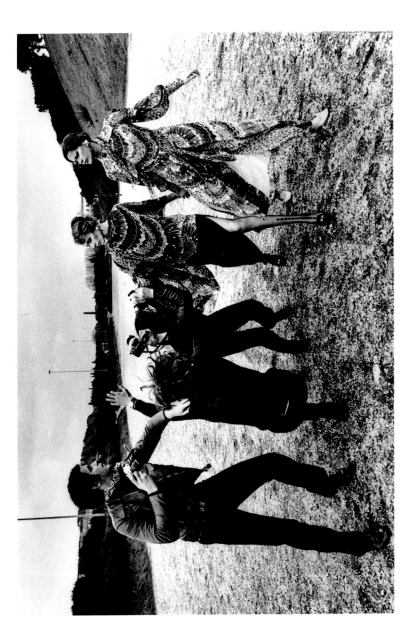

48. *Queen*, 1966. Venice. Frank Usher.

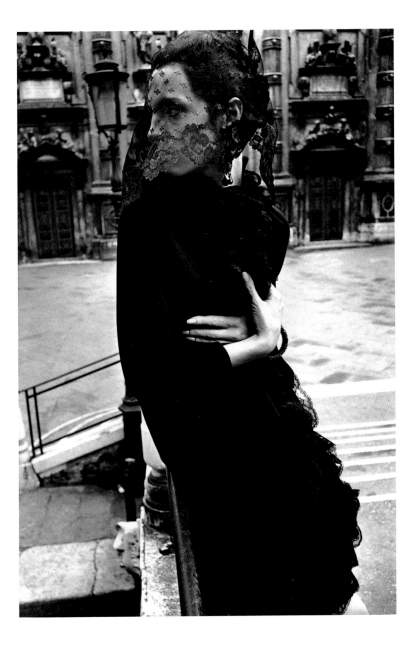

49. *Queen*, 1967. London. National Fur Company.

Overleaf: 50. Countess Vera von Lehndorff, Paris, 1984.

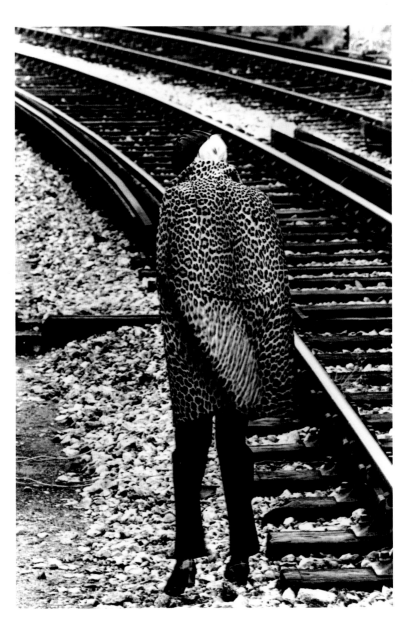

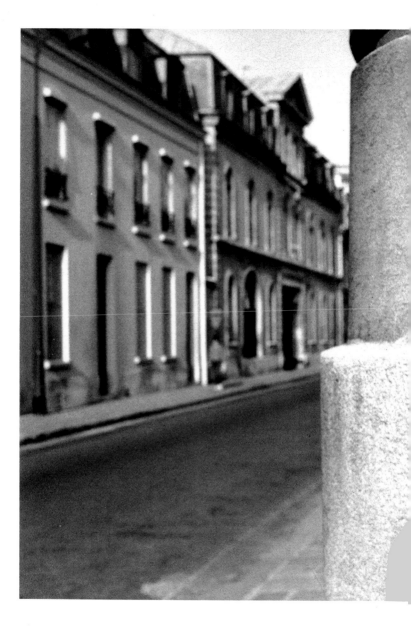

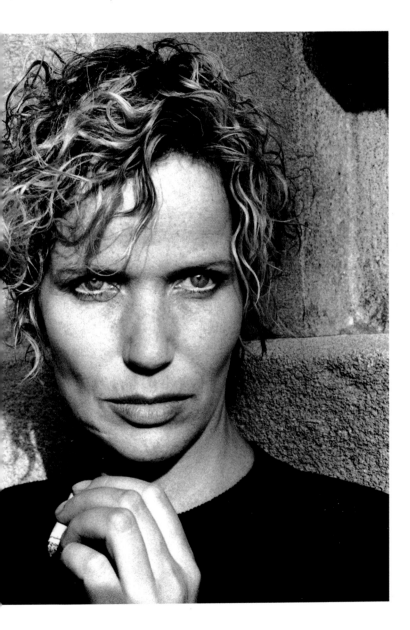

51. Laura dressed in a fox cape, Avenue George V, Paris, 1974.

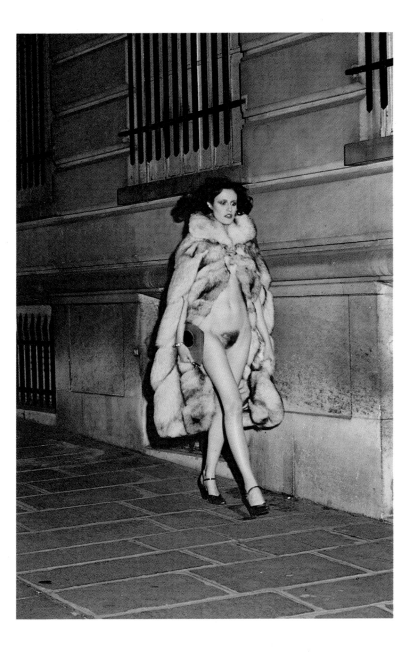

52. Self-portrait, Hotel Due Tori, Verona, 1976.

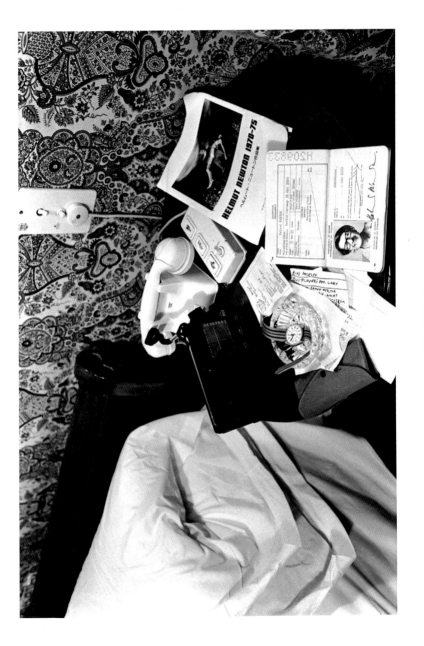

53. Suzy at home, Paris, 1974.

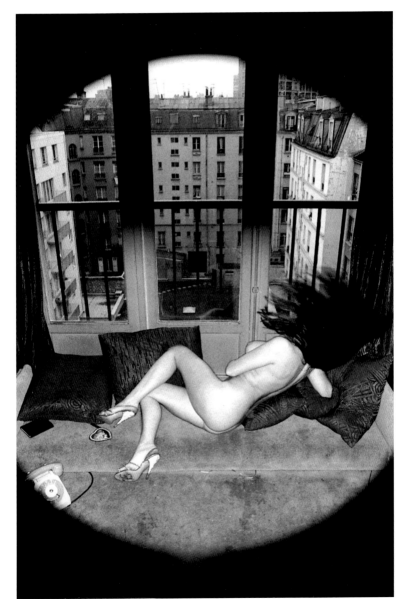

54. Wibeke riding her husband's mechanical bear, Paris, 1975.

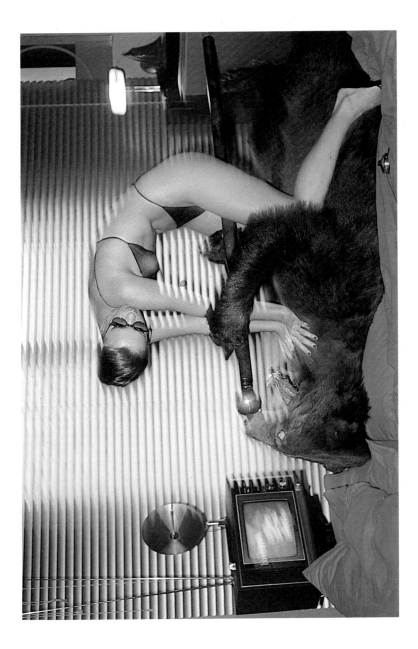

55. Suzy vibrating, Paris, 1974.

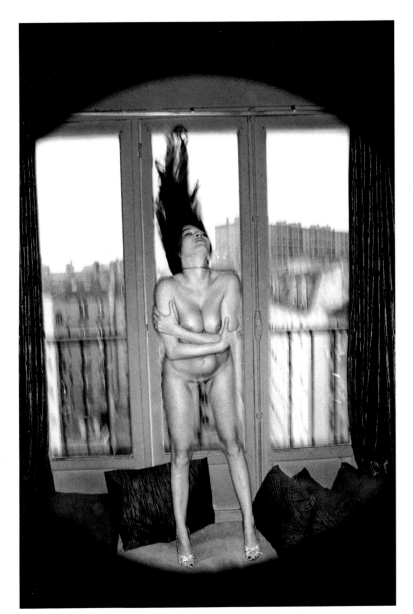

56. Self-portrait, Hôtel Bijou, Paris, 1973.

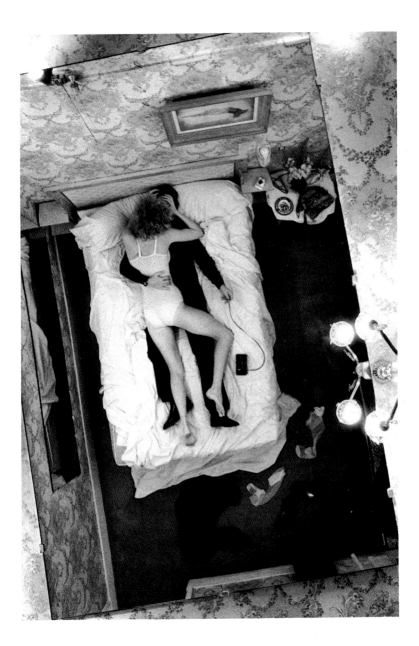

57. 16th arrondissement, Paris, 1975–78.

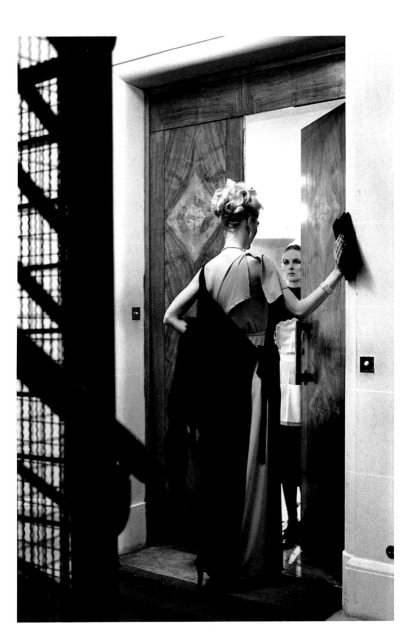

58. Two pairs of legs in black stockings, Paris, 1979.

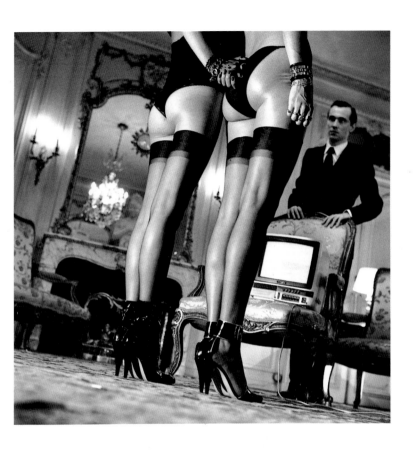

59. *Vogue* (France), 1971. Paris. Givenchy.

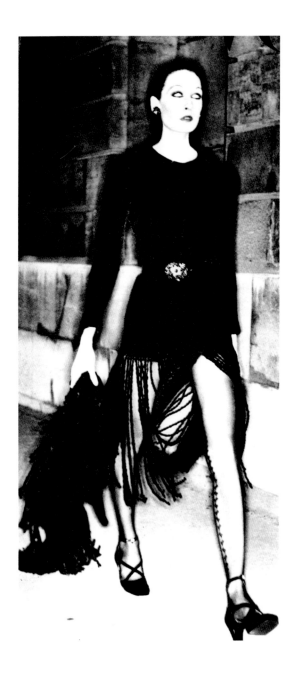

60. *Stern*, 1977. Tuscany, Italy. Karl Lagerfeld for Chloé.

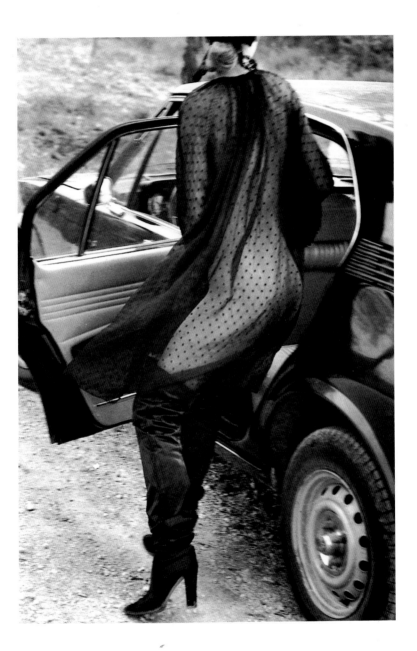

61. For Walter Steiger, 1983. Monte Carlo.

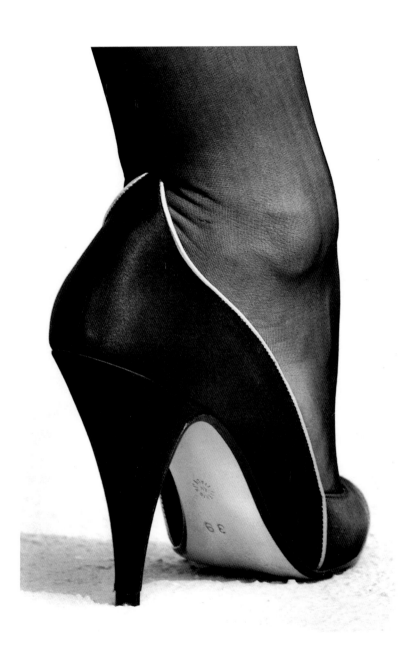

# HELMUT NEWTON BY HELMUT NEWTON

## 1. My Photography

The only thing there is to say about my photos is that they are never blurred! I've always taken pictures, even when I was very young. Photography fascinates me and, in addition, lets me live the way I want to live. I don't consider myself a photographer of the consumer society, but I work in a capitalistic system. I don't claim to produce art either. I've always worked on commission and I'll keep on doing so. With one slight difference over the last 15 years: I always work for others, but now I'm free to choose. That way there's no line between my personal work and what I sell. I don't stash my photos away in drawers. On the contrary – I try to show them to the whole world everywhere. All I can say is that I have full control over my work. I call it making the system work for you. The people who use me have more money than I'll ever see. They are rich – they are industrial leaders, big companies, successful magazines. I don't feel sorry for them. But I also work for free sometimes. And it's just as much fun. I can do photos for magazines put out by young people who don't have enough money to pay the people who work for them. If they're doing something I think is interesting, and if I think I can help them out, then I do it for nothing.

## 2. My Training

I do a lot of portraits which, like nudes, stem from fashion photography, since I've always been a fashion photographer. In the beginning, I wanted to be a big reporter and travel around the world, but it didn't work out that way. When I was 18 I was in Singapore and flat broke. The Singapore *Straits Times* – it's still being published – offered me a job as a reporter. I had a Rolleiflex, but every time there was something to take a picture of, I got there too late. After two weeks they fired me, and for a long time I didn't have any money. My inspiration also comes partly from news photos. I really admire newspaper reporters. In my opinion, news is an exciting field for a photographer. I've studied the work of the paparazzi very closely. For me, their photos are very powerful. I think that photography has been made too intellectual. Especially for beginners, or those who study photography but don't dare push the button.

### 3. The Subject

Q: As a photographer, you are an anti-formalist. Your reaction to fine arts implies that photography must, first and foremost, be the uniqueness of a look at a subject and not only at the form in which the subject is arranged.
A: Absolutely. The subject – that's the big question. That's what I'm interested in.
Q: How do you set up a shot?
A: It's a long process. Something no one knows about is that I do all of my work in writing first. I always carry around a little notebook in which I can jot down the minutest details concerning photos that I'll take some other time. I can't draw. So I make notes on props, lighting, the component parts of my picture. Perspiration under the arms, puffed-up lips, a kiss, a man's shoulder, a woman's hand, the inside of the elbow, the interplay of muscles, man-woman nude to the waist, a man.

### 4. The Message

There is no message in my photos. They are quite simple and don't need any explanation. If by chance they seem a little complex or if you need a while to understand them, it's simply because they are full of details and that a lot of things are happening. But usually they are very simple.

### 5. Staging a Shot

It's the staging that I'm interested in. I also enjoy working at night. For the same reason: to be seen. I'm fascinated by that. Every photographer has his obsession, and that's mine. I'm used to using everything around me. When I take a picture of diamonds, for example – and I like shooting them on a beach in sunlight – I always have trouble with the insurance companies. They don't want you to take a step without a bodyguard. When I took these pictures, the hardest part was showing that these men were armed. The model, the diamonds – they were easy. But I didn't want the bodyguards to notice that they were in the shot. Like a lot of photographers, I am also fascinated by store-window mannequins. I like to lead the viewer on a wild goose chase. Often the models look like mannequins and the mannequins look like humans. The mix-up amuses me, and I like to play on that ambiguity in my photos. Another one of my obsessions is swimming pools. When I was a boy, I competed in sports a lot. I love water, it fascinates me like swimming pools fascinate me, especially the ones in big cities.

## 6. A Special World

The world that I photograph is very particular: there are always, or almost always, the same kind of characters. There are always women, women that are apparently rich. I photograph the upper class because I'm well acquainted with it. And when someone asks me why I never show the other side of the coin, I reply that I don't really know much about it, but that there are other photographers who can do a marvellous job. I prefer to stick with what I know. If I took a picture of models in a poverty-stricken setting, it would be completely false. People have said that my photos have nothing at all to do with reality. That's not true: everything is based on reality.

## 7. Women

I don't work very much in the studio because I think that a woman cannot come to life in front of a white background. I want to show how a woman in a certain milieu lives, the kind of car she drives, her setting, what kind of men she sees. It doesn't matter where they come from – New York, Paris, Nice, Monte Carlo. Their nationality doesn't matter either. The women of a certain milieu, not matter where they're from, all look and dress alike. I am very impressed when I travel from one continent to another, from Paris to Beverly Hills; the women can't possibly resemble each other, but their clothes and make-up are always the same. It's a sign of the consumer society. You can buy Yves Saint Laurent anywhere in the world. I wanted to show the rules of a certain society. It's just bringing out into the open certain types of behaviour.

## 8. Provocation

Q: What does the desire to provoke that so often underlies your work mean?

A: I like and look for reactions. I don't like kindness or gentleness. I want to provoke, but not by choice of subject, although I do need certain subjects in order to create new photographic effects, and especially to find the new visual tension that the choice of these subjects allows me. If I drown a woman in props, or if I pose her like a signpost, if I contrast nudity with clothing, if I ask for a black bra under a light-coloured blouse, I obtain or I'm looking for new interactions of tension which seem surprising and then are accepted. The only provocation that I hate is that of the surrealist image. It has no place in my world.

## 9. Vulgarity

Q: Some works have been published under your name that are not without some vulgarity. How do you react to that?

A: I totally believe in these books. I love vulgarity. I am very attracted to bad taste – it is a lot more exciting than that supposed good taste which is nothing more than a standardized way of looking at things. I am proud of a book like *Sleepless Nights*. A little less of *Secret Women*, which was incredibly successful. I don't practise photography for myself, not for art. If the art world rejects me, all I can say is, 'Good luck to the world of art.' If I look for a real point of view, I'm not going to start by looking at what art will accept so I can conform to that. That's why in *Sleepless Nights* all that sadomasochism still looks interesting to me today. I always carry chains and padlocks in my car trunk, not for me but for my photos – by the way, I never make the knots real tight.

Sections 1, 2, 4, 5, 6 and 7 are taken from a conference given by Helmut Newton in Austria in 1984. Sections 3, 8 and 9 are from an interview with Helmut Newton by Bernard Lamarche-Vadel, in *Artistes*, no. 7, January–February 1981.

# BIOGRAPHY

**1920** Born 31 October in Berlin.

**1930–32** Studies at the Heinrich von Treitschke Realgymnasium in Berlin.

**1933–36** Attends the American School in Berlin.

**1938–40** Apprentice with the fashion photographer Yva in Berlin.

**1938–40** Lives in Singapore.

**1940** Moves to Australia, where he stays for 17 years.

**1940–44** Serves in the Australian army.

**1948** Marries the actress June F. Browne (June Brunell).

**1956** Moves to London for a year, works for *Vogue* UK.

**1957** Moves to Paris. Works with publications *Jardin des modes*, *Elle*, *Queen*, *Playboy*, *Nova*, *Marie-Claire*, *Stern* and various editions of *Vogue*.

**1975** First solo exhibition at the Galerie Nikon, Paris.

**1976** Awarded prize for the best photograph by the Art Directors Club of Tokyo.

**1977–80** Awarded the American Institute of Graphic Arts prize.

**1978–79** Wins the German Art Directors Club gold medal for the best editorial photograph.

**1981** Moves to Monte Carlo.

**1989** Made Chevalier des Arts et Lettres (France).

**1990** Receives the Grand Prix National de la Photographie (France).

**1992** Made Chevalier des Arts, Lettres et Sciences (Monaco).

Between 1976 and 2004, receives many international awards.

**2003** Decides to leave his entire body of work to his hometown of Berlin.

**2004** Dies in a car accident in Hollywood, California, on 23 January, aged 83.

His photographs are included in the following collections:

Stiftung Preussicher Kulturbesitz, Berlin
Editions Condé Nast, Paris and New York
Bibliothèque Nationale, Paris
Musée d'Art Moderne de la Ville de Paris
Musée Chéret, Nice
Musée départemental des Vosges, Epinal
Fashion Institute of Technology, New York
Museum of Modern Art, New York
George Eastman House, Rochester, NY
Nikon Foto Gallery, Zurich
Photographers' Gallery, London
Marlborough Gallery, New York
Xavier Moreau, New York
G. Ray Hawkins Gallery, Los Angeles
John Dunnicliff
Art Directions, Paris

# BIBLIOGRAPHY

## Publications by Helmut Newton

*Femmes Secrètes (Secret Women)*. Text by Philippe Garner. Paris: Editions Robert Laffont; New York: Congreve; London: Quartet; Munich: Rögner und Bernhard, 1976

*Sleepless Nights*. Text by Edward Behr. Paris: Filipacchi; New York: Congreve; London: Quartet; Munich: Schirmer/ Mosel, 1978

*24 Photo Lithos: Special Edition*. Preface by Brion Gysin. Paris: Filipacchi; New York: Congreve; Munich: Rögner und Bernhard, 1979

*Big Nudes*. Preface by Bernard Lamarche-Vadel. Paris: Editions du Regard, 1981

*47 Nudes*. London: Thames & Hudson, 1982

*White Women*. Text by Philippe Garner. Tokyo: Kodansha, 1983

*A World Without Men*. Text by Helmut Newton. New York: Xavier Moreau, 1984

*Helmut Newton: Portraits*. New York: Pantheon; Paris: Nathan; Munich: Schirmer/Mosel; London, Quartet, 1986

*Helmut Newton's Illustrated No 1: Sex and Power*. New York: Xavier Moreau, 1987

*Helmut Newton's Illustrated No 2: Pictures from an Exhibition.* Text by Helmut Newton. Munich: Schirmer/Mosel, 1987

*Helmut Newton: Private Property*. Munich: Schirmer/Mosel, 1989

*Das Glas im kopf wird vom Glas.* Text by Jan Fabre. Ghent: Imschoot Uitgevers, 1990

*Helmut Newton's Illustrated No 3: I Was There.* Text by Helmut Newton. Munich: Schirmer/Mosel, 1991

*Helmut Newton: Pola-Woman.* Foreword by Helmut Newton. Munich: Schirmer/Mosel, 1992

*Immorale*. Tokyo: Kodansha, 1993

*Helmut Newton's Illustrated No 4: Dr. Phantasme*. Munich: Schirmer/ Mosel, 1995

*72 ore a Roma*. Text by Ettore Sottsass. Rome: Peliti, 1998

*Us and Them: Helmut Newton & Alice Springs*. Zurich: Scalo, 1998

*Pages from the Glossies: Facsimiles 1956–1998*. Zurich: Scalo, 1998

*Helmut Newton's Sumo Book*. Cologne: Taschen, 1999

*Helmut Newton: Pour la liberté de la presse*. Paris: Reporters Sans Frontières, 2004

*The Best of Helmut Newton: Selections From His Photographic Work*. Text by Zdenek Felix, Noemi Smolik, Urs Stahel, Munich: Schirmer/Mosel, 2004

*A Gun for Hire*, June Newton, Cologne: Taschen, 2005

*Playboy: Helmut Newton*, Text by Hugh M. Hefner, Walter Abish, San Francisco: Chronicle Books, 2005

## Exhibition Catalogues

*Portraits*. Text by Françoise Marquet. Paris: Musée d'Art Moderne de la Ville de Paris, 1984

*Portraits*. Amsterdam: Foto Foundation, 1986

*Nouvelles Images*. Text by Henri Chapier. Paris: Espace photographique de Paris, Paris Audiovisuel, 1988
*Portraits*. London: National Portrait Gallery; Munich: Schirmer/Mosel, 1988

*Portraits*. Text by Klaus Honnef and Helmut Newton. Tokyo: Metropolitan Teien Art Museum, 1989

*Nuevas Imágenes*. Madrid: Fundación Caja de Pensiones, 1989

*New Images*. Text by Ennery Taramelli and Laura Leonelli. Bologna: Galleria d'Arte Moderna, 1989

*Helmut Newton in Moscow*. Moscow: Pushkin Museum and First Gallery, 1989

*Eroticism in the 20th Century*. Tokyo and Fukuoka: Goro International, sponsored by the Goethe-Institut, Tokyo, and the Photographic Society of Japan, 1992

*Naked and Dressed in Hollywood*. Text by Jan van der Marck. Los Angeles: Pascal de Sarth Gallery, 1992

*Archives de Nuit*. Text by José Alvarez. Paris: Crédit Foncier de France and Editions Hazan, 1992

*Aus dem photographischen Werk*. Texts by Noemi Smolik and Urs Stahel. Hamburg: Deichtorhallen, 1993

*Regards d'artistes sur la femme*. Paris: Hôtel de la Monnaie, 1993

*Vanités*. Paris: Centre national de la photographie, Hôtel Salomon de Rothschild, 1993

*Mes derniers nus*. Paris: Galerie Vallois, 1994

*Helmut Newton: Photography*. Tokyo: Odakyu Museum; Osaka: Navio Museum, 1995

*The Best of Helmut Newton*. Hamburg: Deichtorhallen, 1996

*The Artificial of the Real: Anton Josef Trcka, Edward Weston, Helmut Newton*. Editied by Carl Haenlein. Zurich: Scalo, 1998

## Films

*Helmut Newton*, television documentary by Michael White, Thames Television, London, 55 minutes, 1978

*Frames from the Edge*, television documentary by Adrian Maben, R M Productions, Munich, 90 minutes, 1988

*The Originals*, television documentary, Sleeping Giant Productions, Toronto, 25 minutes, 1992

*Helmut by June*, television documentary by Alice Springs (June Newton) for Canal Plus, Paris, 58 minutes, 1995

# SELECTED EXHIBITIONS

## Solo Exhibitions

**1975** Galerie Nikon, Paris. Canon Photo Gallery, Amsterdam

**1976** The Photographers Gallery, London. Nicolas Wilder Gallery, Los Angeles

**1978** Marlborough Gallery, New York

**1979** American Cultural Center, Paris

**1980** G. Ray Hawkins Gallery, Los Angeles

**1981** Galerie Daniel Templon, Paris

**1982** Studio Marconi, Milan. Gallery Denise René/Hans Mayer, Düsseldorf. Marlborough Gallery, New York. Tanit Gallery, Munich. Photokina, Cologne

**1983** Asher/Faure Gallery, Los Angeles

**1984** Musée Chéret, Nice. Museo Palazzo Fortuny, Venice. *Private Property*, G. Ray Hawkins Gallery, Los Angeles

**1984–85** *Retrospective*, Musée d'Art Moderne de la Ville de Paris

**1985** *New Work*, G. Ray Hawkins Gallery, Los Angeles. *Retrospective*, Museo dell'Automobile, Turin

**1985–86** Galerie Artis, Monte Carlo

**1986** *Retrospective*, Palais de l'Europe, Menton. *Retrospective*, Foto Foundation, Amsterdam

**1987** *Retrospective*, Rheinisches Landesmuseum, Bonn. *Nus inédits*, Galerie Daniel Templon, Paris. *Retrospective*, Groninger Museum, Groningen

**1988–89** *Nouvelles Images*, Paris Audiovisuel, Paris. *Retrospective*, National Portrait Gallery, London

**1989** *Fashion Photographs & Portraits*, Metropolitan Teien Art Museum, Tokyo. *Fashion Photographs & Portraits*, Seibu Art Museum, Funabashi. *Nuevas Imágenes*, Fundación Caja de Pensiones, Madrid. *Helmut Newton in Moscow*, Pushkin Museum and First Gallery, Moscow. *Fashion Photographs & Portraits*, Prefectural Museum of Art, Fukuoka. *New Images*, Galleria d'Arte Moderna, Bologna

**1989–90** *New Images*, Ny Carlsberg Glyptotek, Copenhagen

**1990** Kunstforum, Vienna. Hochschule für Graphik und Buchkunst, Leipzig. *Fashion Photographs & Portraits*, Museum of Modern Art, Shiga

**1991** Biennale, Lyons. Museum of Modern Art, Bratislava. *Naked and Dressed*, Hamilton Gallery, London

**1992** *Naked and Dressed in Hollywood*, Pascal de Sarthe Gallery, Los Angeles. *Helmut Newton*, Goro International Exhibition, Tokyo

**1993** *Helmut Newton*, Galleria Carla Sozzani, Milan. Centre Culturel Française, Rome. *Archives de Nuit*, Villa Medici, Rome

**1993–94** *Helmut Newton aus dem photographischen Werk*, Deichtorhallen Hamburg

**1994** Josef Albers Museum, Bottrop. Fotomuseum Winterthur, Winterthur. Castello di Rivoli, Turin. *Archives de Nuit*, Centro Andaluz de la Fotografía, Almería. Institut Français, Prague. *Mes derniers nus*, Galerie Vallois, Paris

**1989** *Archives de Nuit*, Galerie Pierre Nouvion, Monaco. *Helmut Newton: Photography*, Odakyu Museum, Tokyo. *Nude Works 1992–1995*, Hamilton Gallery, London

**1996** *Helmut Newton: Photography*, Navio Museum, Osaka. *Pulp Fiction*, Galleria Carla Sozzani, Milan. *Helmut Newton*, Artforum Vilka Gallery, Thessaloniki. *Fashion and Fantasy*, Gallery for Fine Photography, New Orleans

**1997** *Helmut Newton: Photography*, Camera Works, Berlin. *Helmut Newton in Sweden*, Hasselblad Foundation at the Gothenburg Museum, Gothenburg

**1998** *72 ore a Roma*, Galleria Comunale d'Arte Moderna e Contemporanea, Rome. *Us and Them: Helmut Newton & Alice Springs*, Museum for Modern Art, Copenhagen; Fotomuseet, Odense

**1999** *Us and Them: Helmut Newton & Alice Springs*, Centre for Contemporary Art, Stockholm; Kunsthal, Rotterdam; Maison Européenne de la Photographie, Paris; Galleria Carla Sozzani, Milan; Josef-Haubrich-Kunsthalle, Cologne

**2003** *Yellow Press*, Galerie Daniel Templon, Paris

**2005** *A Gun for Hire*, Grimaldi Forum, Monaco. *Us and Them*, Helmut Newton Foundation, Berlin. *Sex and Landscapes*, Helmut Newton Foundation, Berlin

**2006** *Helmut Newton's Private Property*, Helmut Newton Foundation, Berlin

## Group Exhibitions

**1975** *Fashion Photography: 6 Decades*. Emily Lowe Gallery, Hofstra University, New York

**1977** *The History of Fashion Photography*. International Museum of Photography, George Eastman House, Rochester, NY

**1979** *La Mode*. Galerie Zabriskie, Paris

**1980** *20/24 Polaroid*. Galerie Zabriskie, Paris, *Instantanés*, Centre Georges Pompidou, Paris

**1981** *Aspects de l'art d'aujourd'hui, 1970–1980*. Musée Rath, Geneva *Hans Bellmer, Helmut Newton, Alice Springs*. G. Ray Hawkins Gallery, Los Angeles

**1982** *50 Années de photographies de Vogue Paris*. Musée Jacquemart-André, Paris; and Photokina, Cologne

**1985** *Shots of Style*. Victoria and Albert Museum, London

**1986** *La femme sur la plage*. Palais de l'Europe, Menton

**1988** *Splendeurs et misères du corps*. Musée de la Mode, Paris; Musée d'Art Moderne, Paris; Triennale Internationale de la Photographie, Fribourg. *The Art of Photography*. Royal Academy of Arts, London

**1989** *The Art of Photography*. Museum of Fine Arts, Houston; Ministry of Culture of the Soviet Union, Moscow; Kunstforum, Vienna

**1991** *Appearances*. Victoria & Albert Museum, London

**1993** *Regards d'artistes sur la femme*. Hôtel de la Monnaie, Paris. *Vanités*. Centre National de la Photographie, Hôtel Salomon de Rothschild, Paris

**1995** Palazzo Grassi, Venice Biennale

**1998** *Josef Trcka, Edward Weston, Helmut Newton,*. Kestner Gesellschaft, Hanover. *67 New Portraits*. Festival Visa pour l'Image, Perpignan

**1999** *Architecture & Pornography*. Castello di Rivoli, Turin